Common abbreviations

c. = cup / fl. oz.= fluid ounce /g. = gram/
gal. =gallon/ Lbs. = pound / kg. = kilogram / L. = liter
ml. = milliliter / oz. = ounce / pt. = pint / qt.=quart
t. or tsp. = teaspoon / T. or Tbsp.= tablespoon

Common conversions

1 tsp. / 5 ml.
1 Tbsp. / 3 tsp. / 1/2 fl. oz. / 15 ml.
2 Tbsp. / 6 tsp. / 1 fl. oz. / 1/8 cup / 30 ml.
4 Tbsp. / 12 tsp. / 2 fl. oz. / 1/4 cup / 60 ml.
1/2 cup / 8 Tbsp. / 24 tsp. / 4 fl. oz. / 120 ml.
1 cup / 16 Tbsp. / 48 tsp. / 8 fl. oz./ 240 ml.
2 cups / 32 Tbsp. / 96 tsp. / 1 pt. / 16 fl. oz. / 75 ml.
4 cups / 64 Tbsp. / 192 tsp. / 2 pt. / 32 fl. oz. /950 ml.
4 quarts or 1 gallon / 3.8 L
1 pint / 500 ml.
1 quart / 0.95 ml.
1 gallon / 3.8 L

Oven temperature

120 c / 250 f
160 c / 320 f
180 c / 350 f
205 c / 400 f
220 c / 425 f
232 c / 450 f

RECIPE : ______________________________

INGREDIENTS

DIRECTIONS

RECIPE : ______________________

INGREDIENTS

DIRECTIONS

RECIPE : ______________________________

INGREDIENTS

DIRECTIONS

RECIPE :

INGREDIENTS

DIRECTIONS

RECIPE : ______________________________

INGREDIENTS

DIRECTIONS

RECIPE : ______________________________

INGREDIENTS

DIRECTIONS

RECIPE :

INGREDIENTS

DIRECTIONS

RECIPE : ___

INGREDIENTS

DIRECTIONS

RECIPE : ______________________________

INGREDIENTS

DIRECTIONS

RECIPE : ______________________________

INGREDIENTS

DIRECTIONS

RECIPE : ______________________________

INGREDIENTS

DIRECTIONS

RECIPE :

INGREDIENTS

DIRECTIONS

RECIPE : ______________________________

INGREDIENTS

DIRECTIONS

RECIPE : ______________________________

INGREDIENTS

DIRECTIONS

RECIPE : ______________________________

INGREDIENTS

DIRECTIONS

RECIPE :

INGREDIENTS

DIRECTIONS

RECIPE : ______________________

INGREDIENTS

DIRECTIONS

RECIPE :

INGREDIENTS

DIRECTIONS

RECIPE :

INGREDIENTS

DIRECTIONS

RECIPE : ______________________________

INGREDIENTS

DIRECTIONS

RECIPE : ______________________________

INGREDIENTS

DIRECTIONS

RECIPE :

INGREDIENTS

DIRECTIONS

RECIPE : ______________________________

INGREDIENTS

DIRECTIONS

RECIPE :____

INGREDIENTS

DIRECTIONS

RECIPE : ______________________________

INGREDIENTS

DIRECTIONS

RECIPE : ______________________________

INGREDIENTS

DIRECTIONS

RECIPE : ______________________________

INGREDIENTS

DIRECTIONS

RECIPE :

INGREDIENTS

DIRECTIONS

RECIPE : ____________________

INGREDIENTS

DIRECTIONS

RECIPE :

INGREDIENTS

DIRECTIONS

RECIPE :

INGREDIENTS

DIRECTIONS

RECIPE : ______________________________

INGREDIENTS

DIRECTIONS

RECIPE : ______________________________

INGREDIENTS

DIRECTIONS

RECIPE :

INGREDIENTS

DIRECTIONS

RECIPE : ______________________________

INGREDIENTS

DIRECTIONS

RECIPE : ______________________________

INGREDIENTS

DIRECTIONS

RECIPE :______________________________

INGREDIENTS

DIRECTIONS

RECIPE : ____________________

INGREDIENTS

DIRECTIONS

RECIPE : ____________________

INGREDIENTS

DIRECTIONS

RECIPE : ______________________________

INGREDIENTS

DIRECTIONS

RECIPE : ______________________

INGREDIENTS

DIRECTIONS

RECIPE : ______________________________

INGREDIENTS

DIRECTIONS

RECIPE :

INGREDIENTS

DIRECTIONS

RECIPE : ______________________________

INGREDIENTS

DIRECTIONS

RECIPE :

INGREDIENTS

DIRECTIONS

RECIPE : ______________________________

INGREDIENTS

DIRECTIONS

RECIPE : ____________________

INGREDIENTS

DIRECTIONS

RECIPE : ____________________

INGREDIENTS

DIRECTIONS

RECIPE : ______________________________

INGREDIENTS

DIRECTIONS

RECIPE :

INGREDIENTS

DIRECTIONS

RECIPE : ______________________________

INGREDIENTS

DIRECTIONS

RECIPE : ______________________________

INGREDIENTS

DIRECTIONS

RECIPE :

INGREDIENTS

DIRECTIONS

RECIPE : ______________________________

INGREDIENTS

DIRECTIONS

RECIPE : ______________________________

INGREDIENTS

DIRECTIONS

RECIPE :

INGREDIENTS

DIRECTIONS

RECIPE : ______________________________

INGREDIENTS

DIRECTIONS

RECIPE :____

INGREDIENTS

DIRECTIONS

RECIPE :

INGREDIENTS

DIRECTIONS

RECIPE : ____________________

INGREDIENTS

DIRECTIONS

RECIPE : ________________________________

INGREDIENTS

DIRECTIONS

RECIPE :

INGREDIENTS

DIRECTIONS

RECIPE : ______________________________

INGREDIENTS

DIRECTIONS

RECIPE : ______________________________

INGREDIENTS

DIRECTIONS

RECIPE : ______________________________

INGREDIENTS

DIRECTIONS

RECIPE : ____________________

INGREDIENTS

DIRECTIONS

RECIPE : ________________________________

INGREDIENTS

DIRECTIONS

RECIPE : ______________________________

INGREDIENTS

DIRECTIONS

RECIPE :

INGREDIENTS

DIRECTIONS

RECIPE : ______________________________

INGREDIENTS

DIRECTIONS

RECIPE : ____________________

INGREDIENTS

DIRECTIONS

RECIPE : ______________________________

INGREDIENTS

DIRECTIONS

RECIPE : ____________________

INGREDIENTS

DIRECTIONS

RECIPE : ____________________

INGREDIENTS

DIRECTIONS

RECIPE :

INGREDIENTS

DIRECTIONS

RECIPE : ____

INGREDIENTS

DIRECTIONS

RECIPE : ____

INGREDIENTS

DIRECTIONS

RECIPE :

INGREDIENTS

DIRECTIONS

RECIPE :

INGREDIENTS

DIRECTIONS

RECIPE : ____________________

INGREDIENTS

DIRECTIONS

RECIPE : ______________________________

INGREDIENTS

DIRECTIONS

RECIPE : ______________________________

INGREDIENTS

DIRECTIONS

RECIPE : ______________________________

INGREDIENTS

DIRECTIONS

RECIPE : ______________________________

INGREDIENTS

DIRECTIONS

RECIPE :

INGREDIENTS

DIRECTIONS

RECIPE : ______

INGREDIENTS

DIRECTIONS

RECIPE :

INGREDIENTS

DIRECTIONS

RECIPE : ______________________________

INGREDIENTS

DIRECTIONS

RECIPE : ______________________________________

INGREDIENTS

DIRECTIONS

RECIPE : ____________________

INGREDIENTS

DIRECTIONS

RECIPE : ______________________________

INGREDIENTS

DIRECTIONS

RECIPE : ____________________

INGREDIENTS

DIRECTIONS

RECIPE :

INGREDIENTS

DIRECTIONS

RECIPE : ______________________________

INGREDIENTS

DIRECTIONS

RECIPE : ____________________

INGREDIENTS

DIRECTIONS

RECIPE : ______________________________

INGREDIENTS

DIRECTIONS

Common abbreviations

c. = cup / fl. oz.= fluid ounce /g. = gram/
gal. =gallon/ Lbs. = pound / kg. = kilogram / L. = liter
ml. = milliliter / oz. = ounce / pt. = pint / qt.=quart
t. or tsp. = teaspoon / T. or Tbsp.= tablespoon

Common conversions

1 tsp. / 5 ml.
1 Tbsp. / 3 tsp. / 1/2 fl. oz. / 15 ml.
2 Tbsp. / 6 tsp. / 1 fl. oz. / 1/8 cup / 30 ml.
4 Tbsp. / 12 tsp. / 2 fl. oz. / 1/4 cup / 60 ml.
1/2 cup / 8 Tbsp. / 24 tsp. / 4 fl. oz. / 120 ml.
1 cup / 16 Tbsp. / 48 tsp. / 8 fl. oz./ 240 ml.
2 cups / 32 Tbsp. / 96 tsp. / 1 pt. / 16 fl. oz. / 75 ml.
4 cups / 64 Tbsp. / 192 tsp. / 2 pt. / 32 fl. oz. /950 ml.
4 quarts or 1 gallon / 3.8 L
1 pint / 500 ml.
1 quart / 0.95 ml.
1 gallon / 3.8 L

Oven temperature

120 c / 250 f
160 c / 320 f
180 c / 350 f
205 c / 400 f
220 c / 425 f
232 c / 450 f

Lightning Source UK Ltd.
Milton Keynes UK
UKHW020632040221
378234UK00013B/1195

9 781777 561512